Creepy, Crawly
Baby Bugs

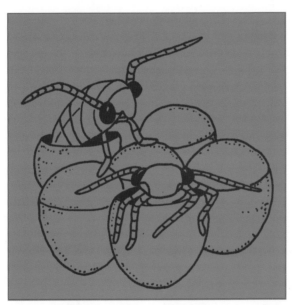

Sandra Markle

Walker and Company
New York

For Dr. Fred Sherberger, whose fascination with creepy, crawly bugs is inspirational.

The author wishes to express appreciation to Philip P. Parrillo, collections manager, Division of Insects, Field Museum of Natural History, Chicago, Illinois; to Dr. Curtis Gentry, Fernbank Science Center, Atlanta, Georgia; and to my assistant, Constance Parramore; for sharing their expertise and enthusiasm.

First published in the United States of America in 1996 by Walker Publishing Company, Inc.

Published simultaneously in Canada by Thomas Allen & Son Canada, Limited, Markham, Ontario

Library of Congress Cataloging-in-Publication Data
Markle, Sandra.
Creepy, crawly baby bugs/Sandra Markle.
p. cm.
Includes index.
Summary: Offers a close look at baby insects, those animals which are nicknamed "bugs."
ISBN 0-8027-8443-7 (hardcover). —ISBN 0-8027-8444-5 (reinforced)
1. Insects—Infancy—Juvenile literature. [1. Insects. 2. Animals—Infancy.] I. Title.
QL467.2.M3625 1996
595.7'039—dc20   95-47178
                                                    CIP
                                                    AC

Line art on pages 30 and 31 by the author.

Book design by Janice Noto-Helmers

Printed in Hong Kong

2 4 6 8 10 9 7 5 3 1

Words that appear in blue in the text are included in the glossary.

Note: For anyone interested in learning more about the insects in this book, each is identified in the photo credits with as much of the following information as possible: order, family, species, and the name of the person who named it. This identification is supplied by Philip P. Parrillo, collections manager, Division of Insects, Field Museum of Natural History, Chicago, Illinois.

PHOTO CREDITS

Title page: Brush-footed butterfly caterpillar (Lepidoptera: Nymphalidae). *Tom Myer*

Page 3. Giant silk moth caterpillar (Lepidoptera: Saturniidae). *Rudie Kuiter*

Page 4. Giant water bug nymph (Hemiptera: Belostomatidae: *Belostoma* sp.). *Dwight Kuhn*

Page 5. Aphid (Homoptera: Aphididae). *Dwight Kuhn*

Page 6. Walnut caterpillars (Lepidoptera: Notodontidae: *Datana integerrima* [Grote and Robinson]). *Tom Myers*

Page 7. Zebra butterfly caterpillar (Lepidoptera: Heliconiidae: *Heliconius charithonius* [Linnaeus]). *Brian Kenney*

Page 8. Monarch butterfly caterpillar (Lepidoptera: Danaidae: *Danaus plexippus* [Linnaeus]). *Kenneth Lorenzen*

Page 8. Monarch butterfly chrysalis (Lepidoptera: Danaidae: *Danaus plexippus* [Linnaeus]). *Kenneth Lorenzen*

Page 9. Monarch butterfly adult (Lepidoptera: Danaidae: *Danaus plexippus* [Linnaeus]). *Kenneth Lorenzen*

Page 10. Praying mantis nymphs (Mantodea: Mantidae: *Stagmomantis septentrionalis* [Saussure and Zehntner]). *Ken Preston-Mafham*, Premaphotos

Page 12. Parasitic wasp larvae (Hymenoptera: Braconidae: *Apanteles glomeratus* [Linnaeus]) emerging from the caterpillar of the large white butterfly (Lepidoptera: Pieridae: *Pieris brassicae* [Linnaeus]). *Ken Preston-Mafham*, Premaphotos

Page 13. Giant water bug nymph (Hemiptera: Belostomatidae *Belostoma* sp.). *Dwight Kuhn*

Page 14. Io moth caterpillar (Lepidoptera: Saturniidae: *Automeris io* [Fabricius]). *Brian Kenney*

Page 16. Honeybee eggs and larvae (Hymenoptera: Apidae: *Apis mellifera* [Linnaeus]). *Kenneth Lorenzen*

Page 17. Honeybee larvae (Hymenoptera: Apidae: *Apis mellifera* [Linnaeus]). *Kenneth Lorenzen*

Page 18. Oakblue butterfly caterpillar (Lepidoptera: Lycaenidae: *Narathura* sp.); Green tree ants (Hymenoptera: Formicidae: *Oecophylla smaragdina* [Fabricius]). *Ken Preston-Mafham*, Premaphotos

Page 19. European earwig (Dermaptera: Forficulidae: *Forficularia auricularia* [Linnaeus]). *Chris Timmins*

Page 20. California silk moth caterpillar (Lepidoptera: Saturniidae: *Hyalophora euryalus* [Boisduval]). *Edward Ross*

Page 22. Inchworm (Lepidoptera: Geometridae). *Maria Zorn*

Page 23. Elephant hawk moth caterpillar (Lepidoptera: Sphingidae: *Deilephila elpenor* [Linnaeus]). *Ken Preston-Mafham*, Premaphotos

Page 24. Fungus gnat larva (Diptera: Mycetophilidae: *Arachnocampa* sp.). *Ken Preston-Mafham*, Premaphotos

Page 25. Spittlebug nymph (Homoptera: Cercopidae: *Philaenus* sp.). *Dwight Kuhn*

Page 26. Caddisfly nymph (Trichoptera: Limnephilidae: *Discomoecus* sp.). *Edward Ross*

Page 27. Cicada adult emerging (Homoptera: Cicadidae: *Venustria superba* [Goding and Froggatt]). *Ken Preston-Mafham*, Premaphotos

Page 28. Honeybee pupae (Hymenoptera: Apidae: *Apis mellifera* [Linnaeus]). *Kenneth Lorenzen*

Page 29. Adult worker honeybee emerging (Hymenoptera: Apidae: *Apis mellifera* [Linnaeus]). *Kenneth Lorenzen*

The little claws on the ends of its feet help this giant silk moth larva hold on and pull itself along.

You may not have seen a baby bug that looks just like this one. But baby bugs can be spotted crawling across the ground or on leaves. They can be found hiding under rocks—and even in ponds and puddles. So how does a baby bug live? How does it stay safe? And what kinds of changes happen as it grows up? This book will let you take a close look at baby insects—those animals nicknamed "bugs."

Two Ways to Start Life

All baby insects develop inside eggs. Some females lay their eggs and leave them. Others care for the eggs until they hatch. Giant water bug eggs are tended—but not by Mom. When the female lays her eggs, she produces a special glue. Unable to reach her own back, she sticks the eggs to her mate. He then pushes water over the eggs from time to time with his back legs. This helps the developing babies get the oxygen they need from the water.

Giant water bug babies hatching.

4

An aphid is born.

HEAD

THORAX

ABDOMEN

Still other female insects, like aphids, keep the eggs inside their bodies until the babies hatch. In this way the mother provides protection, and the young get the food they need from the egg yolk.

Take a close look at the mom and you'll see the special features most baby bugs will have when they grow up. Adult insects usually have three main body parts: a head; a thorax, or middle section; and an abdomen, or hind end. They also have six legs, and an exoskeleton— or supporting frame—outside rather than inside the body.

Getting Bigger

Just look at these walnut caterpillars eat! That's what baby bugs do most of the time. No wonder farmers think many baby bugs are pests.

As the caterpillars eat, their toothed-edged jaws move against each other like scissors, snipping off leafy bites.

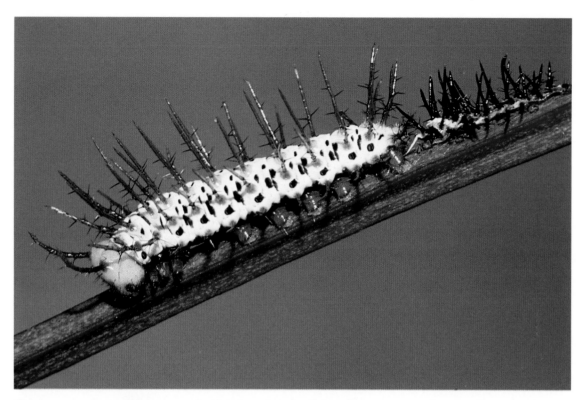

Some caterpillars eat their shed skin, but most just move on, leaving it behind.

All this eating helps the babies grow. But their tough outer layers don't give them room to get bigger. So the baby bug's body gives off special juices that loosen this coat from the soft inner layers. The exoskeleton splits open, and the larva molts, or sheds its skin. Now the youngster can expand in size by swallowing air or water. Then the outer layer hardens and darkens again. Most baby bugs molt a number of times as they grow up.

Two Ways to Grow Up

Some insect babies, like the monarch butterfly caterpillar, grow up in stages: larva, pupa, and adult. The larva eats and grows. The pupa doesn't eat, and during this stage the baby's body structure and systems change to those of the adult. Some adults, like this monarch, eat. Others, who live for only a short time, never eat. All adults mate and produce more babies. These insect babies are also born without the developing wings, or wing buds, that some have.

larva

The monarch caterpillar is eating milkweed, its favorite food.

The caterpillar spun a silken pad. Then, hanging upside-down from the pad, it shed its skin one last time.

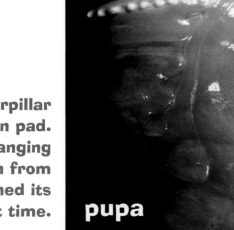

pupa

Hungry animals that have once tasted a monarch leave others alone. The adult's bad taste comes from special chemicals in the milkweed the caterpillars ate.

adult

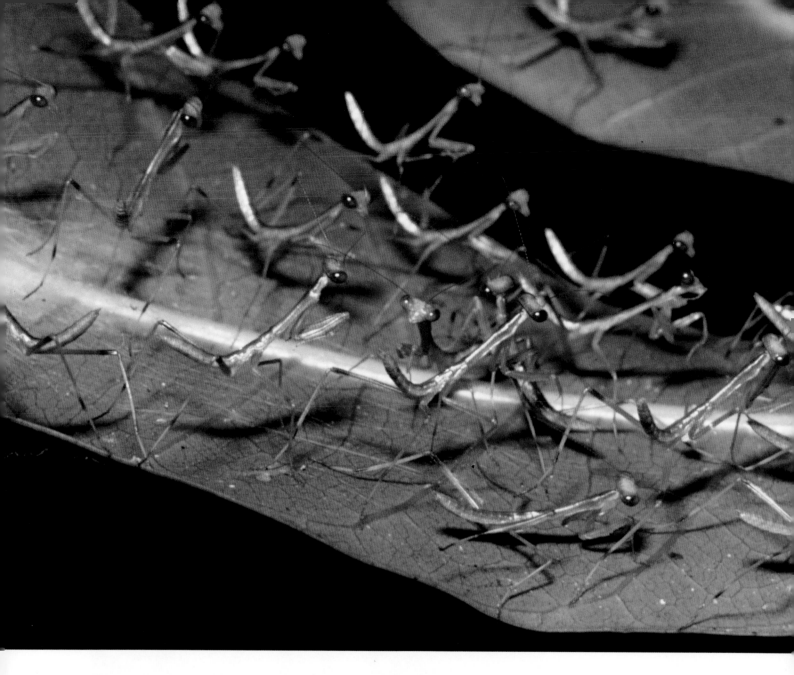

So many praying mantis babies emerging
all at once means at least a few will
escape being eaten by hungry animals.

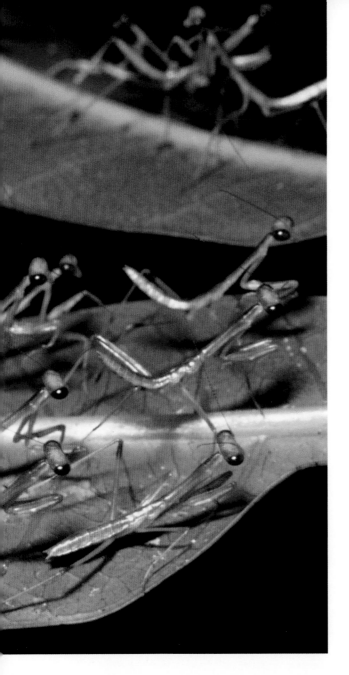

Other insect babies, like praying mantis babies, have tiny wing buds from the time they hatch. They often eat the same sort of food as the adults and may even look like tiny adults. Most important, they never go through a pupal stage. This kind of baby bug is called a nymph.

The praying mantis nymphs are all together because they just hatched. Soon, they'll go off on their own.

On Their Own

The baby wasps are bursting through a caterpillar's exoskeleton. Their mother injected her eggs into the caterpillar and left. When the larvae hatched, they ate the caterpillar's body parts and grew. Now they will go through the pupal stage and change into adults. Then they will mate, and the females will go searching for caterpillars in which to lay their eggs.

If you don't like sharing your room with a brother or sister, imagine these baby wasps all living inside one caterpillar!

12

Like all insects called "true bugs," the baby giant water bug has piercing-sucking mouthparts.

This giant water bug nymph doesn't have any trouble catching food for itself with its clawed front feet. Next, it stabs its beaklike mouthparts into the fish and squirts in some special juices. These juices change the fish's insides into a soft goo—perfect baby food for the nymph to slurp up.

14

The io caterpillar's head is tucked to shield it.

Some baby insects are equipped to defend themselves. This io moth caterpillar is curled up in its "don't touch me" position. The yellow-green tufts are sharp spines that give off a poison that makes its enemies' skin sting and raises an itchy bump. Imagine what it would be like for a bird to swallow one of these caterpillars!

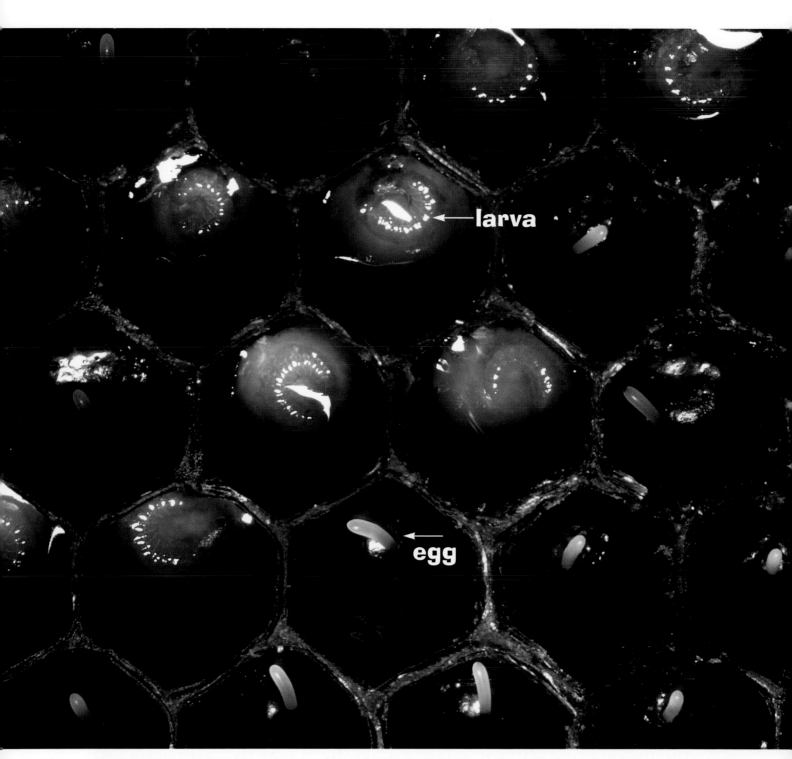

larva

egg

The bluish white honeybee larvae are curled up like crescent moons. What look like little white tubes are honeybee eggs that haven't hatched yet.

Taking Care of Baby

· ·

Baby honeybees have a whole colony of workers to take care of them. The bluish white larvae are one-day-old honeybees. They are each in a pool of milky liquid food called royal jelly. This is supplied by the worker bees from special body parts in the head. Larvae become new workers if their food is switched after three days to a mixture of honey and pollen, special grains produced by flowers. Larvae treated like princesses and fed royal jelly for six days grow up to be queens. Only queens are able to mate and lay eggs.

These are honeybee larvae after about five molts. When they're ready to change into pupae, workers cap the cells with wax.

Being green helps this caterpillar stay safe.

Don't worry. The green tree ants swarming over this oakblue caterpillar aren't attacking it. They're drinking a sweet liquid it gives off especially to attract the ants. And the ants act like living armor, shielding the caterpillar from wasps that might lay eggs on it. So, in fact, the ants and the caterpillar are partners, helping each other.

18

Imagine having thirty brothers and sisters to bug you! Some earwigs do. They also have a devoted mother. A female earwig rarely leaves her brood. After the eggs are laid, she picks them up in her mouth, one by one, to clean them. And she stays with the young after they hatch, guarding and cleaning them. Once the babies have molted one or two times, they go off on their own.

The ovals are earwig eggs that haven't hatched yet. The pale babies will get darker with future molts.

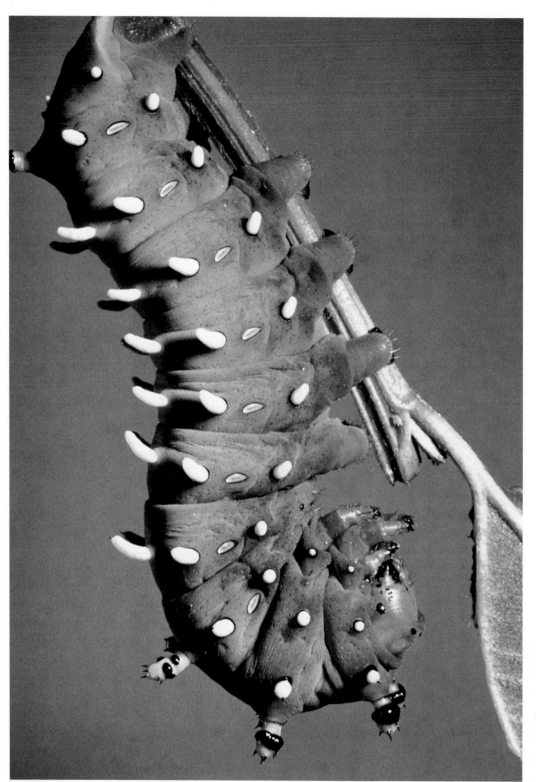

Silk comes out of
a little tube on the
caterpillar's head,
and it moves its
head from side to
side to spin its
cocoon.

Tricky Babies

· ·

This California silk moth caterpillar is green to let it blend in with the leaves, but take a close look. You'll see the parts most caterpillars have.

Its eyes are tiny dots arranged in a crescent. It probably doesn't see more than light or dark. But it has parts that stick out around its mouth to help it smell and feel the world around it.

Each white oval down its sides has a slit in the middle. These are the openings through which the caterpillar breathes.

The three pairs of short clawlike legs just below its head let the caterpillar hold on to a leaf while it eats. And there are five more pairs of fleshy limbs that are like extensions of its body. These end in tiny hooks that let the caterpillar cling to plants.

Look at the inchworm pretending to be a twig. It's spun a silk thread to help it balance.

Caterpillars have lots of muscles to help them move and, in this case, stretch out straight as a stick.

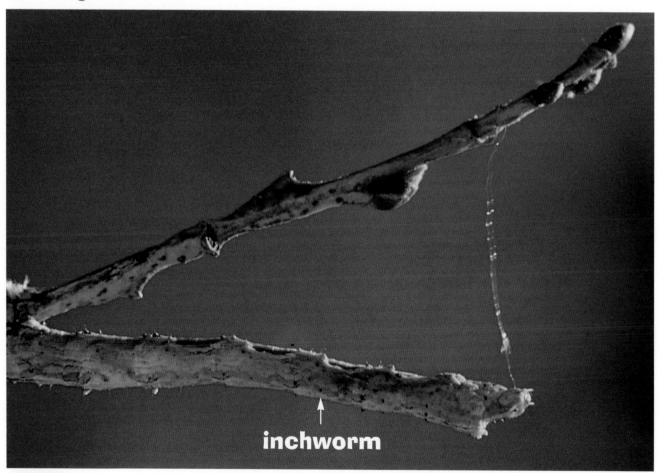

inchworm

The caterpillar's head is really below the part with the eyespots.

The elephant hawk moth caterpillar is playing another sort of trick. Big spots on its back mimic a snake's eyes. When threatened, the caterpillar may also rear its body into the air and twist violently from side to side. It may even click its jaws to act fierce.

larva

This long, brown, wormlike larva is the baby of a tiny gnat that lives mainly in the Waitomo Caves in New Zealand.

Imagine growing up covered in slime! This tricky gnat larva uses the slimy liquid it produces in its mouth to build a tube nest. And it dangles down more clear, sticky strands—some as long as a human adult's forearm. Because the larva glows, the strands appear to glow too. If the larva is lucky, an insect will fly into one of these strands and become stuck. Then the larva contracts its body again and again to pull up the sticky strand and its meal.

24

Home Alone

Spittlebug nymphs make bubble nests that they hide inside. Wondering how? The young bug feeds by sucking juice from plants. Some of this juice passes through its body and oozes as bubbles from openings on its abdomen. The bubbles don't burst easily, so they quickly pile up. Before long, the nymph is completely covered with bubbles.

Wondering why this bug is called a spittlebug? Watch in the mirror while you push your tongue against your teeth several times, making bubbles of spit ooze out of your mouth.

The bubbly blob keeps away hungry ants that might eat the spittlebug. It also keeps the bug from drying out.

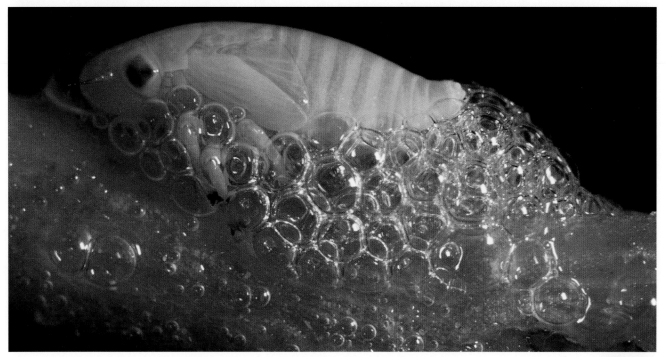

The caddisfly's house is really only about the size of the end joint of your little finger.

This caddisfly larva stays safe in the underwater house it built for itself. The house is made of sand grains stuck together with waterproof glue and silk produced by special body parts in the baby bug's head. When danger threatens, the larva pulls back inside its house. A little hole at the tail end of the case helps keep water flowing over the larva's gills, body parts that take in the oxygen the young insect needs. When it's hungry, the larva stretches out and goes searching for food—tugging its mobile home along.

Becoming an Adult

After the cicada nymph hatched from an egg laid on a tree branch, it dropped to the ground. Then it tunneled down to the tree's roots. It stayed in the ground, sucking the tree's juices and growing slowly. Ready to become an adult, it emerged from the ground and molted. Now, as soon as its wings expand and stiffen and its body darkens, the adult cicada will fly in search of a mate. Within weeks, new eggs will be laid, and the adult will die.

An adult cicada emerges.

27

Here the wax caps on the cells have been removed to let you peek inside at the honeybee pupae.

Honeybees go through a pupal stage as they grow up. Look back at the larvae on page 17 to see how different they look as pupae. During this stage, all of their body systems change too. Large, dark, compound eyes and three simple eyes show pupae closest to becoming adults. When the changes are completed, the adult chews through the wax cap and crawls out. Like all baby bugs that survive to grow up, this bee is now ready to start its adult life.

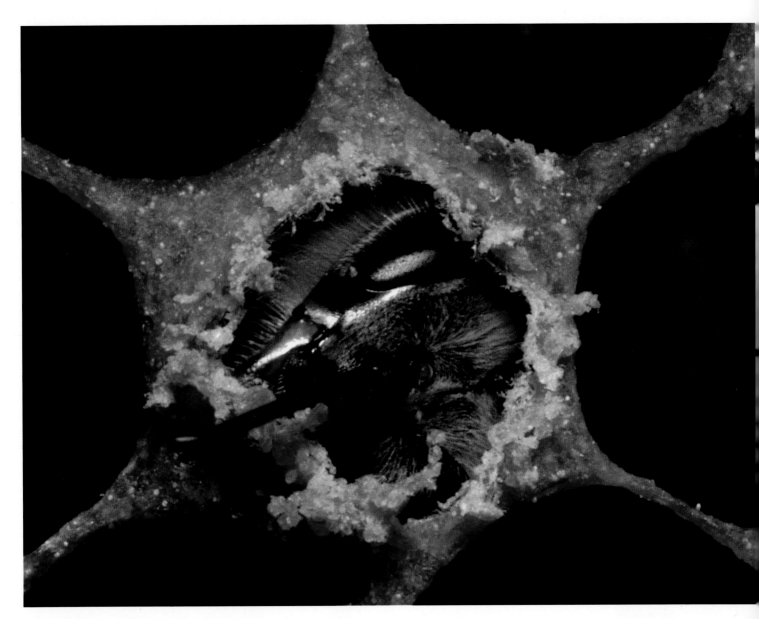

An adult worker bee emerges.

Glossary/Index

ə as in banana
ä as in father
ā as in day
ē as in beat
ī as in side
ȯ as in saw
ō as in bone
ū as in rule
ng as in sing
ˊ indicates a stressed syllable

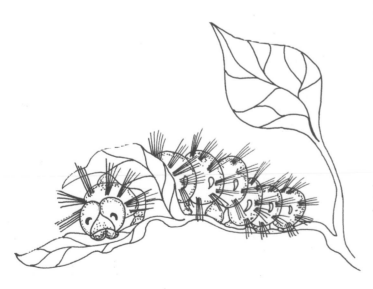

Inchworm 22

Io Moth Caterpillar 14-15

Larva (ˊlär-və) The name given to insect young that go through a pupal stage and have their body structure change as they become adults. 7, 8, 12, 17, 26, 28 (plural: larvae [ˊlär-vē])

Molt (mōlt) To shed old skin. 7

Monarch Butterfly 8-9

Nymph (nimpf) Name given to insect young that don't pass through a pupal stage. 11, 13, 25, 27

Oakblue Caterpillar 18

Pollen (ˊpä-lən) Special grains produced by flowering plants as part of their reproductive process; insects and other animals sometimes use this as food. 17

Praying Mantis 10-11

Pupa (pyüˊpə) Nonfeeding stage between larva and adult. During this stage the body structure and systems change into those of an adult. 8, 28 (plural: pupae [pyüˊpē])

Royal Jelly (ˊroi-ell)(ˊje-lē) A food produced in special body parts in the heads of honeybee workers and fed to the larvae. All larvae are given this for three days; those that become queens are fed royal jelly throughout their development. 17

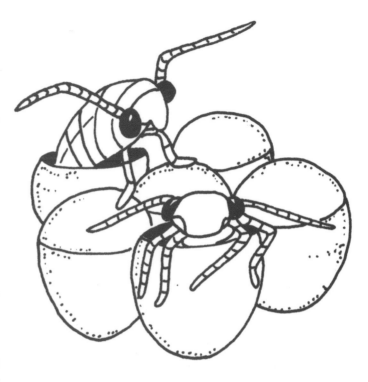

Spittlebug 25

Thorax (ˊthor-aks) Body region between the head and abdomen that bears the wings and legs if these are present. 5

True Bugs (ˊtrü)(bugz) Group of insects that all share certain features, including piercing-sucking mouthparts and having young that are nymphs. 13

Walnut Caterpillar 6

Wasp 12, 18

Wing Buds (ˊwing)(ˊbədz) Developing wings that are visible on some nymphs. These grow larger with each molt. 8, 11

Things to Do

Track Down Baby Bugs If you would like to watch caterpillars or larvae in action, look for the plants that are their favorite foods. Here are a few to search for: common milkweed, cabbage, kale, tomatoes. Caterpillars and larvae like many types of trees too. Look for baby insects underneath leaves as well as on top. If you have a camera, take it along. Then when you find a caterpillar or larvae to observe, you can also take a picture. Make notes about what the young insect is doing and what it's eating. Put the notes and photos in a scrapbook. Scrapbooks make the best collections—they are easier to store and the insects are left alive in the wild.

Go Galling Galls are lumps and bumps on leaves and stems. Although some are caused by mites or even fungi, most form when the larva of certain kinds of flies and wasps bores into a plant. Special chemicals from the larva cause the plant to grow abnormally, forming a bump. Inside this bump, the larva eats the plant material around it. You could say that the larva grows up eating its house.

Find a gall on a plant in late spring or early summer. Tie a bright-colored strip of cloth on the plant so you can find it again easily. Measure the gall every week or so to see how much it grows. Watch for a tiny hole to appear. (It will probably be next spring.) That means the baby bug has grown up and moved on. Then cut open the gall to see the inside of this bug's plant house.